# A PET WHAT?!

# PYGMY GOAT

Karen Latchana Kenney

Rourke
Educational Media

rourkeeducationalmedia.com

*Scan for Related Titles
and Teacher Resources*

## Before & After Reading Activities

## Before Reading:

### Building Academic Vocabulary and Background Knowledge

Before reading a book, it is important to tap into what your child or students already know about the topic. This will help them develop their vocabulary, increase their reading comprehension, and make connections across the curriculum.

1. *Look at the cover of the book. What will this book be about?*
2. *What do you already know about the topic?*
3. *Let's study the Table of Contents. What will you learn about in the book's chapters?*
4. *What would you like to learn about this topic? Do you think you might learn about it from this book? Why or why not?*
5. *Use a reading journal to write about your knowledge of this topic. Record what you already know about the topic and what you hope to learn about the topic.*
6. *Read the book.*
7. *In your reading journal, record what you learned about the topic and your response to the book.*
8. *After reading the book complete the activities below.*

### Content Area Vocabulary
*Read the list. What do these words mean?*

bond
breeders
disbudding
domesticated
forage
herd
kids
mammal
predators
ruminants
vaccinations
vegetarian
veterinarian

## After Reading:

### Comprehension and Extension Activity

After reading the book, work on the following questions with your child or students in order to check their level of reading comprehension and content mastery.

1. *Where should pet pygmy goats live? (Summarize)*
2. *Why do you think some owners remove their pygmy goat's horns? (Infer)*
3. *What food do pygmy goats forage for? (Asking questions)*
4. *Do you think a pygmy goat would be a good pet for your family? Why? (Text to self connection)*
5. *What might happen if you don't take care of a pygmy goat's hooves? (Asking questions)*

### Extension Activity
Pygmy goats are domesticated animals. Pick another kind of domesticated animal to research, such as a cow, horse, dog, or cat. What wild animal is its ancestor? When did humans domesticate this animal?

# Table of Contents

# Happy Kids

It's morning on the farm and two young pygmy goats are ready for some fun! The cute **kids** jump onto a tree stump, wagging their tails. Then they hop off, kicking their legs high into the air.

**FUN FACT**

Kids just practice head butting. But for adults, head butting shows strength and power in a **herd**.

They stand up on their hind legs. They fall forward and butt heads. But the kids aren't hurt. They're just playing. Pygmy goats love to play and explore. Their cute looks, small size, and playful personalities make them popular pets.

Pet pygmy goats come from **breeders**. But this small animal originally came from West Africa.

A pygmy goat is a **domesticated** animal. Its distant relative is the wild Bezoar goat. People trained wild goats to be tame over thousands of years. That's how they became farm animals.

*wild Bezoar goat*

**FUN FACT**
Goats can live 10 to 14 years. The oldest known goat lived more than 22 years!

The pygmy goat is also called the Cameroon Dwarf Goat. It comes from the country of Cameroon. Herds are now in many parts of West Africa. In West Africa, the pygmy goat is raised mostly for its meat, but it also makes milk. The first pygmy goats to leave Africa went to zoos in Sweden and Germany. They first came to the United States in 1959.

Africa

West Africa

# Pygmy Goats: Head to Toe

⟨ horns

unusual eyes ⟩

thick hair ⌄

tough teeth ⟩

What's so cute about pygmy goats? They're not just tiny. They have short legs, a big forehead, and a large, round body. They look like baby goats even as adults. They grow to just 16 to 22 inches (41 to 56 centimeters) tall. That's about the size of a dog. This small **mammal** also has many other unique features.

hooves ⟩

**Horns:** Two bony horns grow from a pygmy goat's head. Horns help keep goats cool by letting off body heat. Goats also protect themselves from **predators** with their horns.

**Thick Hair:** Pygmy goats have medium to long, straight hair. It gets thicker in colder areas or seasons. Males have long, full beards and a mane.

**Hooves:** Hard hooves have two toes. Hooves make pygmy goats great climbers.

**Tail:** Its short tail sticks up and wags back and forth.

**Tough Teeth:** Pygmy goats chew a lot of tough plants. They have grinding teeth in the back of their mouths. At the front, they only have teeth on their lower jaw. The top jaw just has hard gums at the front.

**Unusual Eyes:** A goat's eye pupils aren't round. They're rectangular! This lets them see far at the sides of their head while eating plants by the ground.

‹tail

# Pet Pygmies

Why would you pick a goat as a pet? Pygmy goats have unique, playful personalities. They're easy to care for, and they get along well with people and other animals.

Some owners walk their pet pygmy goats on leashes, just like dogs. These pets **bond** well with owners. They love to cuddle. Some even sit on their owners' laps.

# Nigerian Dwarf Goats

You can choose another kind of miniature goat as a pet. A Nigerian Dwarf goat is cute too. It looks like a regular goat, just much smaller. It is a dairy goat. That means it needs to be milked at least twice a day.

 *Some Nigerian Dwarf goats have splotchy spots or large stripes.*

Playful goats should live outdoors. They need space to roam with plants and sticks to nibble on. Before you decide a pygmy goat is right for you, make sure they are allowed where you live. Check with your local government office to find out if there are any restrictions.

## Pet Pointers

It's a good idea to talk with your neighbors before deciding to make pygmy goats part of your family. Goats can be noisy. Some people don't like the smells or sounds goats make.

These herd animals need to live with other goats, so it's best to get at least two. If you have other animals, that helps. They can keep your pygmy goat company. Your pet will be much happier.

You may want to pick female pygmies. Males can be harder to care for. They pee on their legs and beards. They try to attract females. They can be a little smelly. But a neutered male mixes well with female goats. It doesn't try to attract them.

Horns can be a problem too. Pygmy goats may get excited and accidently poke you, causing a serious injury. Goats can also destroy fences. Some owners choose to remove their pet's horns. This is called **disbudding**, which must be done when pygmy goats are only two weeks old.

You can buy a pygmy goat from a breeder. Ask the breeder about the goat's health and find out what **vaccinations** it has had. A goat rescue farm is another great option. These goats may have been neglected or abused. Or their owners couldn't afford to keep them. Adopt a pygmy goat to give it a new chance at having a happy home.

▲▲ *A pygora is a mix of a pygmy goat and an Angora goat. It was bred for its coat, which is full and curly.*

# Caring for Your Pet Pygmy

Pygmy goats need a big area enclosed by a good fence. Goats are great at escaping. Build a fence at least 4 feet (1.2 meters) tall. Use wooden posts and wire mesh.

Your pet pygmy needs a dry, draft-free outdoor shelter that lets in fresh air. Solid wood is best. Goats like to chew on things and chemicals might be in other materials.

A 6-by-8-foot (1.8-by-2.4-meter) shed fits two pygmy goats. Line the floor with straw or wood shavings. A bench makes a nice bed for a pygmy goat. Put a concrete or paved area by the shed. Pygmy goats don't like to get muddy. They can stand on the hard area to stay dry and clean.

# A Healthy Diet

A pygmy goat is a **vegetarian**. It mostly eats grass and alfalfa hay. Goats also **forage** for food. They chew on tree bark, brush, dry leaves, and weeds. Make sure their home is free of poisonous plants. Tulips, acorns, and oak trees are a few things that can poison goats.

These clean animals like their food to be clean too. Never put it on the ground. Make a raised eating area for your pets. Hang a feedbag from a fence. Or build a feeder that keeps food off the ground. Make sure your pets have fresh, clean water every day.

## Pet Pointers

You may need to give your pet extra vitamins or minerals. Depending on where you live, these nutrients might be missing from your hay. Check with your **veterinarian**.

Please do not feed the pygmy goats they are on a special diet.

▲▲ *Goats are **ruminants**. This means they have four stomachs, which slowly break down the plants they eat. Goats chew and swallow food, bring it back up to chew once more, and swallow it again. Then it moves through their stomachs.*

A pygmy goat's hooves grow like fingernails. They need to be trimmed every four to six weeks. If they get too long, your goat will limp. Its feet will hurt. It might get hoof rot, an infection of the hooves. Use hoof trimmers to make hooves flat.

Does your goat look sick? Is it thin? Is it coughing? It might have worms in its intestines. That's common in goats. You need a good veterinarian for your pet. Make sure your pet gets the vaccinations and care it needs to stay healthy.

## Pet Pointers

Sometimes goats eat too much grain or spring grass, which can lead to bloat. This is a buildup of gases in its stomachs. Your goat's left side will bulge. It's very serious. Without treatment, bloat could kill your pet.

If it's not used to people, a pygmy goat can be a nervous pet. Spend as much time as you can with your goats. This is especially important when you first bring them home.

Try quietly reading a book to your goats. Take them into their shed at night and put them to bed. Bring them some hay to eat. Pet your new friends. They will start to know you. They will be comfortable around other people, too.

One of the best parts about being a pygmy goat owner is watching your pets play! Make them a playground. Give your goats lots of things to climb up, jump off, and run around. Old tractor tires and logs are great. Make a teeter totter with a board and a log. A trampoline is fun too. Just make sure the springs are covered so your goats won't hurt their legs.

Teach your pets some simple tricks. Train them to shake hands, spin in a circle, or weave between your legs. Give your goats healthy treats as rewards.

## Pet Pointers

**Healthy goat treats include:**

- raisins
- popped popcorn
- sunflower seeds
- chopped apples and pears

Pygmy goats make wonderful pets. They're always curious and playful. They are loving friends to other animals and people. And they're fun to watch! Give your pygmy goats enough space to roam. Build them a nice home. They will become your new best friends!

# Things to Think About If You Want a Pygmy Goat

- **Pygmy goats can be noisy and smelly. Your neighbors might not like them living next door.**

- **Different cities and states have laws about keeping pygmy goats. Make sure it is okay where you live.**

- **You need to own at least two pygmy goats. They do not do well as single pets.**

- **It is important to have space outside for your pets. Pygmy goats need a dry shelter and fenced area to roam.**

- **Owners should trim their goats' hooves every four to six weeks.**

# Glossary

**bond** (BOND): to form a close connection

**breeders** (BREED-urz): people who keep, mate, and sell animals

**disbudding** (diss-BUDD-ing): removing the horns from goats

**domesticated** (duh-MESS-tuh-kate-id): tamed to live with or be used by humans

**forage** (FOR-ij): to search for food

**herd** (HURD): a large group of animals

**kids** (KIDZ): young goats

**mammal** (MAM-uhl): a warm-blooded animal with a spine, whose females produce milk for their young

**predators** (PRED-uh-turz): animals that hunt other animals for food

**ruminants** (ROOM-ih-nuntz): animals that have more than one stomach and chew and swallow food, bring it back up to chew once more, and then swallow it again

**vaccinations** (VAK-suh-nay-shunz): shots given to animals to prevent diseases

**vegetarian** (vej-uh-TER-ee-uhn): an animal that only eats plants

**veterinarian** (vet-ur-uh-NER-ee-uhn): a doctor who treats sick animals

# Index

# Show What You Know

1. Why do adult pygmy goats butt heads?
2. Where do pygmy goats originally come from?
3. How do horns keep pygmy goats cool?
4. What size shed fits two pygmy goats?
5. How should you care for a pygmy goat's hooves?

# Websites to Visit

www.marylandzoo.org/animals-conservation/mammals/pygmy-goat

http://southwickszoo.com/exhibit/pygmy-goat

www.taytopark.ie/zoo/pygmy-goat

# About the Author

Karen Latchana Kenney is an author and editor in Minneapolis, Minnesota. She has written dozens of books for kids on many topics, from how stars and galaxies form to how to care for pet sugar gliders. Her award-winning books have received positive and starred reviews in *Booklist*, *School Library Connection*, and *School Library Journal*. When she's not researching and writing books, she loves biking and hiking Minnesota's state parks, traveling to new and exciting places with her husband and son, and gazing up at the night sky in northern Minnesota at her family's cabin, where the stars are vividly bright.

Visit her online at http://latchanakenney.wordpress.com

**Meet The Author!**
www.meetREMauthors.com

PHOTO CREDITS: Cover © Semmai; title page © Fielding Piepereit; page 4 © jctabb; page 5 © anetapics; page 6 © Shmizia; page 8 © Andrea Huber; page 10 © imageBROKER/Alamy; page 11 © KAdams66, Sharon Foelz; page 13 © SashFoxWalters; page 14 © pathdoc; page 15 © labrynthe, Peeranat Thongyotee; page 16 © MoniqueRodriguez; page 17 © DSchoenigh, cosmonaut; page 18 © jatrax; page 19 © FLPA/Alamy; page 20 © Pete Gallop; page 21 © T.M.O. Pets/Alamy; page 22 © KiraVolkov; page 23 © Mark Hartfield; page 24 © Mark Andrews/Alamy; page 25 © Trevor Hunt; page 26 © Anne Connor, senkaya; page 27 © Asier Romero; page 28 © Nature Picture Library/Alamy; page 29 © GlobalP

Edited by: Keli Sipperley
Cover and interior design by: Rhea Magaro-Wallace

Pygmy Goat / Karen Latchana Kenney
(You Have a Pet What?!)
ISBN 978-1-68342-177-1 (hard cover)
ISBN 978-1-63432-243-3 (e-Book)
Library of Congress Control Number: 2016956537

Printed in the United States of America,
North Mankato, Minnesota

**Library of Congress PCN Data**

**Also Available as:**

ROURKE'S
e-Books